Plunge into the Playful World of

DOLPHINS &
PORPOISES

Published by Wildlife Education, Ltd.
12233 Thatcher Court, Poway, California 92064
contact us at: 1-800-477-5034
e-mail us at: animals@zoobooks.com
visit us at: www.zoobooks.com

ISBN 1-888153-49-0

Dolphins & Porpoises

Series Created by
John Bonnett Wexo

Written by
Beth Wagner Brust

Scientific Consultant
Sam Ridgway, D.V.M., Ph.D.

Contents

Dolphins and porpoises are popular with everyone. Their lively leaps and built-in grins make them easy to love. And their playful curiosity and cleverness make them fascinating to watch.

Swift and acrobatic swimmers, dolphins are the mischief-makers of the sea. They love to play! And they'll play with almost anything—from feathers to sea turtles to people! Bottlenose dolphins are the dolphins most often seen in movies, on television, and in aquatic parks. Because they are the dolphins most frequently kept in captivity, more is known about them than about other dolphins and porpoises.

Dolphins and porpoises are whales, or *cetaceans*. But they are *toothed* whales. This separates them from other, much larger whales that have brush-like baleen instead of teeth. Names can be confusing. Some dolphins are called porpoises, some porpoises are called dolphins, and some dolphins are called whales. Killer whales and pilot whales are the largest of the dolphins, but are still much smaller than the baleen whales. What all this means is that although they come in different shapes and sizes, dolphins and porpoises and some other toothed whales are closely related.

Dolphins and porpoises, like all whales, are *mammals*. They have lungs and must breathe air. They are warm-blooded and their babies are born alive and feed on milk from their mothers. Like all mammals, they have hair at some time in their lives. In the toothed whales, the whiskers around their mouths are lost soon after birth.

Dolphins and porpoises spend most of their time underwater, so they are still a mystery. But studies of wild saltwater dolphins show they form groups numbering thousands of animals.

The sociability of dolphins often extends to humans. For centuries, dolphins have befriended people, and people have honored dolphins in art and literature. Today, millions of people visiting marine parks have seen the affection between dolphins and their handlers and have learned about the dolphin's nature, intelligence, and abilities. Perhaps that is why so many people want to protect dolphins and porpoises from fishing nets, pollution, and other manmade dangers. Once people learn about them, they want to make sure that dolphins will be around for centuries to come.

BOTTLENOSE DOLPHINS

How can you tell a dolphin from a porpoise? It's not as easy as you might think. Dolphins and porpoises are very closely related, they look and act very much alike, and the names dolphin and porpoise are often used interchangeably. But, as you will see, there *are* some small differences between them. Probably the best way to tell these two mammals apart is by the shape of their heads—porpoises usually have smaller heads than dolphins, and they have shorter snouts.

Altogether, there are 25 kinds, or species, of saltwater dolphins, 5 species of freshwater dolphins, 6 species of porpoises, and 6 species that belong to the dolphin family (Delphinidae) but are commonly called whales. Freshwater dolphins are found only in a few large rivers in Asia and South America. But saltwater dolphins and porpoises live all over the world—a few are even found in polar waters. Dolphins do not migrate great distances like large whales. But some do travel hundreds of miles in search of food.

SPOTTED DOLPHIN
Stenella frontalis

To make things even more confusing, there is also a fish called a dolphin! This fish is also known as dorado or mahi-mahi. Like all fish, the dolphin fish is cold-blooded and breathes through its gills. The dolphin mammal is warm-blooded and breathes air with its lungs.

STRIPED DOLPHIN
Stenella caeruleoalba

GANGES RIVER DOLPHIN
Platanista gangetica

The Ganges River dolphin, or *susu*, is a freshwater dolphin found in India and Bangladesh. Almost blind, the susu uses its long snout to probe for food along the river bottom.

COMMON DOLPHIN
Delphinus delphis

HOURGLASS DOLPHIN
Lagenorhynchus cruciger

DALL'S PORPOISE
Phocoenoides dalli

HARBOR PORPOISE
Phocoena phocoena

One way to tell a porpoise from a
dolphin is by the *shape* of its teeth.
Most porpoises, like this harbor
porpoise, have flat, triangular teeth.
Also, all but one kind of porpoise
have triangular fins on their backs.

BOTTLENOSE DOLPHIN
Tursiops truncatus

Dolphins have round, cone-shaped teeth.
Scientists can tell the age of a dolphin or
porpoise by counting the rings on the inner
part of its teeth. Like the rings on a tree,
each ring in the tooth represents one year.

AMAZON RIVER DOLPHIN
Inia geoffrensis

The Amazon River dolphin,
or *boutu*, is the largest of the
freshwater dolphins. It has a
long powerful beak and about
30 large teeth on each side of
its upper and lower jaws.

IRRAWADDY DOLPHIN
Orcaella brevirostris

The Irrawaddy dolphin is named for one of the rivers where it occurs,
although it is not confined to rivers. These dolphins sometimes move out
to sea and have been seen from the Bay of Bengal to northern Australia.

*I*t's hard to believe, but scientists say that the long-ago ancestor of dolphins and porpoises was a *land* mammal that returned to the sea. What's easy to see is that dolphins and porpoises are completely adapted to life in the water. They have sleek, smooth skin lined with *blubber* for warmth. They have broad flippers and tails to help them move through the water. And they have only one nostril—at the top of the head—so they can breathe at the surface without having to expose much of their bodies.

Because they breathe air, dolphins and porpoises have to be able to see in the air and in water. They can do this because their eyes are flexible. Strong muscles around the eye are used to change the shape of the eye's lens for underwater viewing and for looking above the surface. Their large pupils let them see in deep water, but the pupils can be closed to tiny slits so they can see in bright light.

The *dorsal fin* on a dolphin's back may help the animal keep its balance as it swims. Sailboats have a similar structure, called a *keel*, to keep them from tipping over.

KEEL

DORSAL FIN

Dolphin skin is very smooth and firm. It feels rubbery to the touch. A dolphin's skin helps it slide through the water with very little effort.

All the power for pushing a dolphin forward comes from its muscular tail. The end of the tail spreads out into two wide *flukes*. To move through the water, a dolphin pushes the flukes up and down.

Like submarines, dolphins are tapered at the front and back ends—so that water flows easily over the whole body. There are no flat surfaces to slow the animal down.

Dolphins can dive under the water, but they must always come up again for air. They breathe through a nostril called a *blowhole*. Unlike people, who breathe automatically, dolphins have to know *when* to breathe so water doesn't get into the blowhole.

When diving, dolphins always close their blowholes to keep water from getting into their lungs—just as you hold your nose when you dive. To close its blowhole, a dolphin uses powerful muscles on the top of its head.

Like all whales, dolphins have a clear, jelly-like substance in their eyes that looks like tears. This substance keeps the salt from irritating their eyes as they swim underwater.

FLIPPER

HUMAN HAND

Scientists study and compare the anatomy, teeth, organs, tissues, and cells of many living animals and fossil animals. This is how they learn about relationships between animals. This method also helps them determine what an animal's ancestors were like.

Dolphins use their flippers to *steer* through the water. The flippers are firm and smooth and look like pointed paddles. But inside, there are five sets of bones—just like your fingers. To help dolphins move faster in the water, the skin around the "fingers" is fused together to form one smooth surface.

MODERN DOLPHIN

*S*ome dolphins and porpoises feed at night. Others feed during the day. Although fish and squid are their favorite foods, dolphins may also hunt other kinds of prey. These toothed whales also have wonderful senses to help them survive in the water. They have no sense of smell as we know it, but through taste they can detect a variety of *chemicals* in the water. They have no external ears, but they can "hear" above water and underwater. Like bats, they rely on *echolocation*. This ability to use sound waves, or *sonar*, enables them to navigate and to find food or spot danger in murky water, where it's hard to see anything.

When feeding at the surface, some dolphins will leap out of the water to catch a flying fish!

If you stood across from a tall building and shouted "hello," a faint "hello" would probably come back to you as an echo.

HELLO!

HELLO! HELLO!

HELLO! HELLO!

HELLO! HELLO!

Dolphins and porpoises use echoes to help them find food—but instead of words, they make a clicking sound. The clicks hit whatever is around them and then bounce back to the dolphins. Dolphins can send as many as *2,000 clicks per second!*

CLICK! CLICK! CLICK!

FISH! FISH! FISH!

Some scientists compare the dolphin's brain to a computer because it can process so many clicks so quickly. *In just one second*, a dolphin can learn all about an object—its size, shape, speed, and direction. A dolphin's sonar is so sensitive, it can detect a fish the size of a minnow from *10 feet away!*

1

Dolphins often work as a team to catch fish. **1** First, they herd a school of fish into a tight group.

Some dolphins have figured out an easier way to get their next meal. They follow fishing boats and wait for trash fish to be dumped overboard. Or they follow other boats that dump garbage that attracts fish. Then they feed on the fish.

Bottlenose dolphins sometimes whack fish with their tails to send them soaring through the air. When the fish lands in the water again, it is so stunned that it is easy to catch.

2 Then they circle the fish to keep them corralled. Each dolphin takes a turn swimming into the middle to feed.

Dolphins and porpoises sometimes become stranded on the beach and die. Stranding can occur for any number of reasons that might cause physiological stress and disorientation. Whether it's pollution, lack of food, or other trauma, the *stress* weakens the immune system and lets diseases take over. By the time the animals are stranded, they are usually sick, and their "internal compasses" no longer work.

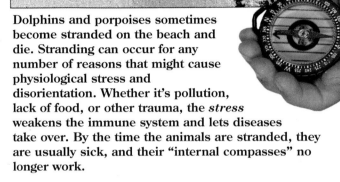

NASAL CAVITY

MELON

INNER EAR

Dolphins focus their sonar the same way a miner focuses his flashlight beam.

To find food, a dolphin sends out a series of clicks. The sound starts in air sacs in the nasal cavity. Then it moves forward through a structure in the dolphin's forehead called the *melon*. The echoes from the fish bounce back and travel through the lower jaw to the inner ear.

2

Once a dolphin catches a fish, it turns it around and swallows it head first! Dolphins have very sharp teeth. But they use their teeth only for grabbing and holding the fish, not for chewing it.

Spotted dolphins get their spots when they are adults. Can you tell the young dolphins from the adults in this picture?

Dolphins and porpoises are social animals and gather in groups of all sizes. River dolphins may be solitary or occur in small groups, while harbor porpoises usually roam coastal waters in small groups of two to five members. Bottlenose dolphins also maintain small units of two to ten animals, but these sometimes merge with other family groups to form a community of as many as a thousand or more individuals. Dolphins that occupy the open ocean form large societies that number in the thousands. These dolphins hunt together, cooperate to herd their prey, and generally help one another to survive.

Dolphins and porpoises are thought to communicate through a mix of sound, body movements, and postures. Above the water, dolphins open their mouths and make creaky-door sounds or high-pitched squeals. Below the water, they click and make many sounds that are too high for humans to hear.

Dolphin calves stay with their mothers for three to six years. At birth, they weigh 30 to 50 pounds and are 35 to 50 inches long. They are toothless for several weeks.

Dolphins make a lot of different noises. They squeak, whistle, whine, groan, and clap their jaws. Sometimes they even sound like they are laughing! No one knows for sure if any of these sounds are used for communication.

Dolphins have been known to help other dolphins that are ill or injured. In such cases, the healthy dolphins swim on either side of the weak one, supporting it with their flippers so that it can breathe.

Dolphins often swim together in formation, like marching soldiers. The *navigating formation* is a wedge with the young protected at the center.

Dolphin mothers are devoted to their babies—and are very protective. Young dolphins can swim away quickly and get lost or be attacked by sharks. So their mothers keep them close at all times. If a baby strays too often, its mother will trap it between her flippers, or she may hold it underwater for some seconds.

The *parade formation* can be an open circle, a square, or a single-file line. Dolphins use this formation when swimming on the open sea.

In the *hunting formation*, dolphins divide into small groups to help each other hunt.

Like lions and elephants, female dolphins serve as "aunties" to help protect the babies from danger. They often work together, forming "playpens" around their young by swimming in a circle. This lets the babies play together in safety.

Large schools of dolphins and porpoises are sometimes sighted out on the open sea. Once, hundreds of thousands of dolphins were seen off the New Zealand coast. As they swam, a tremendous rushing sound could be heard from miles away!

Dolphins are among the most playful of all animals, even as adults. They play with each other, with whatever they may find, and with the fish they are about to eat. They even like to play with people, which may be why people enjoy dolphins so much.

Dolphins learn human games quickly, and they also make up their own games and teach them to people. But mostly, dolphins love to frolic. They leap and somersault out of the water, and they body surf through the waves alongside human surfers—just for the fun of it!

Most dolphins love to ride and leap in the waves created by ships moving through the water. While riding these waves, dolphins can go *more than 35 miles per hour* without even moving their tails!

In some parts of the world, wild dolphins swim right up to the shore to play with people. But as friendly as these dolphins can be, it's still important for people to be cautious when playing with them.

Scientists still have much to learn about dolphins and porpoises. Dolphins and humans have large brains with many folds. Because of this, many people assume that cetaceans are highly intelligent and that their brains are similar to the human brain. Actually, the folding pattern of a dolphin's brain more closely resembles the brain patterns of hoofed mammals.

People have admired dolphins and porpoises since the beginning of civilization. This ancient Greek mural was painted *more than 3,000 years ago*! It is one of the earliest known examples of dolphins in art.

No one knows why dolphins push people or objects toward the shore, but they have done it many times. During World War II, a group of American airmen were stranded in a raft when two dolphins came along and pushed them toward land.

Dolphins will play with almost anything—balls, feathers, driftwood, seaweed, and even their food when they are full. They also play with other sea animals—turtles, fish, seals, birds, and whales—whether the other animals want to play or not!

Even though dolphins have flippers instead of hands, they still use tools—another sign of intelligence. For example, they use coral reefs as a tool to catch fish. They corner the fish inside the barrier, then dart in to feed.

For thousands of years, people in Brazil have depended on dolphins to help them catch fish. When a school of fish approaches, the dolphin makes a splash in the water. Then the fisherman throws in his net. The dolphin eats the fish that don't get caught in the net.

There are many threats to dolphins and porpoises. Two of the greatest threats are pollution and people.

In the eastern tropical Pacific Ocean, tuna swim with dolphins. Because of this, dolphins are often caught in the nets of commercial tuna fishermen. In 1973, 144,000 dolphins died in fishing nets. But by 1993, the dolphin deaths from fishing were down to 3,605. Why the big drop in numbers? The Marine Mammal Protection Act and other protective laws forced the commercial fisheries to change their fishing techniques to reduce dolphin deaths. Nets were modified, observers were put on fishing vessels to monitor the dolphin catch, and divers and the crews of small boats now surround the area of the catch to help release any dolphins caught in the nets.

In the United States, efforts are being made to further protect these animals. As yet, there are no effective international controls.

Killer whales sometimes hunt dolphins for food. When they do, the dolphins bunch together. The whales then swim around them in circles, trapping them in the same way that dolphins trap fish.

Two of the freshwater dolphins—the susu of India and the baiji of China—are close to extinction. There is such tremendous pollution in the rivers where they live that the few dolphins left are barely surviving.

Industrial pollution and the tons of garbage dumped into the ocean may be affecting the dolphin population. In Europe, a whole population of harbor porpoises was wiped out when industrial chemicals were dumped into the sea.

Sometimes sharks attack young dolphins. When this happens, the adult dolphins quickly surround the shark and take turns ramming its soft underbelly with their hard snouts. Sharks have no bones in their bodies, just cartilage—so it's usually the dolphins that win these battles.

Without assistance, when a porpoise or dolphin gets caught in a fisherman's net, it often dies. Sometimes, fishermen who inadvertently net a dolphin don't even try to save it.

The net used to catch tuna is called a purse-seining net. When fish swim into the net, a string is pulled at the bottom to trap them inside. Under the Marine Mammal Protection Act, vessels of the United States fishing fleet help dolphins escape the nets.

WHAT YOU CAN DO!

People can make a difference. When people demanded dolphin-safe tuna, processing plants refused to accept tuna caught without safeguards to protect dolphins. You can help by writing letters to your congressmen. Tell them it's important to keep oceans clean and pollution free. Ask them to convince the International Whaling Commission to include small whales—dolphins and porpoises— in IWC management plans. For more information, write to the National Marine Fisheries Service, 1335 East-West Hwy, Silver Spring, MD 20910, and to the Center for Marine Conservation, 1725 DeSales Street N.W., Washington, D.C. 20036.

If you ever come across a stranded dolphin or porpoise, here's what you should do:

1) If the animal is on its side, prop it up so that it can breathe.

2) Put wet cloth or paper towels over the body and the exposed eyes to protect them from sand and sun. Be sure to keep the tail flukes, dorsal fin, flippers, and head wet—because they give off the most heat. Do NOT get water in the blowhole.

3) Call the nearest stranding network or aquatic park for a rescue.

4) If possible, float the animal into shallow water. Again, you *must* keep the blowhole clear. If too much water gets into the blowhole, the dolphin will drown.

21

For centuries humans have enjoyed the friendliness of dolphins and been inspired to create legends, relate stories, and honor them in art. The ancient Greeks even named a city for the dolphin. Delphi means "dolphin town."

Dolphins were believed to bring good luck to travelers. Certainly this was true for a minstrel and poet named Arion, who lived in the 7th century B.C. Arion was traveling by ship when he was robbed by sailors and thrown overboard. Dolphins rescued the poet and carried him to shore.

Early stories tell of friendships between dolphins and children. In one tale, a dolphin waited for a boy, morning and night, to give him a dolphin-back ride across a lagoon, on the way to and from school. An ancient Greek scholar noted the dolphin's friendliness to humans and that dolphins met ships to "play, frisk, and gambol before them." In more modern times, a dolphin named Pelorus Jack met every large ship that entered the sound between New Zealand's two main islands. Pelorus Jack swam about six miles with each ship and continued to greet ships for almost 24 years!

Today, large commercial fisheries pose a threat to dolphins and porpoises, and legislation is required to protect them. But fishermen in ancient times thought it was a bad omen to kill dolphins. It was like "biting the hand that feeds you," because dolphins drove the fish into the fishermen's nets. Those early fishermen never harmed the dolphins and set them free if they got tangled in the nets. Such cooperation between dolphins and fishermen is still seen in many cultures today.

In Australia, one group of indigenous people still fish as they have for centuries. When the fishermen spot a school of fish, they run to the water and beat the surface with their spears. Dolphins hear the spears smack the water, and they drive the fish toward shore. After the fishermen net their catch, the dolphins eat the remaining fish.

Joint fishing between man and dolphin also occurs with river dolphins. Amazonian Indians protect the boutu because it is their friend and drives the fish to their canoes. In India, the susu is considered sacred and herds fish into the fishing nets. Chinese legend long protected the baiji against harm from people, because it, too, drove fish toward the fisherman.

Today, dolphins still appear in art, books, on coins, and on television and movie screens. They continue to inspire and entertain. But today, we also try to learn more about them so the future will always be filled with dolphins.

SPOTTED DOLPHINS

Index